D1258096

Date: 9/27/16

**J 356.167 SLA**
**Slater, Lee,**
**Delta Force /**

PALM BEACH COUNTY
LIBRARY SYSTEM
3650 SUMMIT BLVD.
WEST PALM BEACH, FL 33406

# DELTA
# FORCE

LEE SLATER

Checkerboard
Library

An Imprint of Abdo Publishing
abdopublishing.com

# abdopublishing.com

Published by Abdo Publishing, a division of ABDO, PO Box 398166, Minneapolis, Minnesota 55439.
Copyright © 2016 by Abdo Consulting Group, Inc. International copyrights reserved in all countries.
No part of this book may be reproduced in any form without written permission from the publisher.
Checkerboard Library™ is a trademark and logo of Abdo Publishing.

Printed in the United States of America, North Mankato, Minnesota
102015
012016

THIS BOOK CONTAINS
RECYCLED MATERIALS

Cover Photo: Shutterstock
Interior Photos: AP Images, pp. 8-9; Corbis Images, pp. 4, 5, 29; Giancarlo Casem/US Army,
p. 15; Grant Probst/US Navy, p. 26; Keating (Capt) No 1 Army Film & Photographic Unit, p. 7; Russell
Roederer/US Army, p. 11; Shutterstock, pp. 13, 14, 17, 19, 21, 25, 27, 29; Thomas Cieslak/US Army,
p. 16; US Army, pp. 6, 10, 24, 28

Content Developer: Nancy Tuminelly.
Design: Anders Hanson, Mighty Media, Inc.
Editor: Liz Salzmann

Library of Congress Cataloging-in-Publication Data
Slater, Lee, 1969-
   Delta Force / Lee Slater.
      pages cm. -- (Special ops)
   Includes index.
   ISBN 978-1-62403-968-3
1.  United States. Army. Delta Force—Juvenile literature. 2.  United States. Army—Commando troops--
Juvenile literature.  I. Title.
   UA34.S64S568 2016
   356'.16--dc23
                      2015026587

# CONTENTS

# THE HUNT FOR THE
# ACE
## OF SPADES

In 2003, the United States led an invasion of Iraq. One of the mission's goals was to find and capture Saddam Hussein. Hussein was a ruthless dictator. Those who did not agree with him were **imprisoned**, tortured, and killed. He was responsible for the deaths of thousands of Iraqi citizens. With Hussein in power, the Iraqi people could not be free.

Saddam Hussein

Hussein had followers who supported his ideas and carried out his plans. To help US soldiers identify these enemies, military leaders created a special deck of cards. Hussein was pictured on the ace of spades. That meant he was the number one enemy. Each of the other cards showed one of Hussein's followers. The mission to capture or kill Hussein was called Operation Red Dawn.

Delta Force soldiers played an important role in Operation Red Dawn. They worked with other special operations professionals to gather information. They arrested suspects and interviewed them. Finally, one of Hussein's trusted friends gave away his hiding place. The hunt was nearly over.

On December 13, 2003, Saddam Hussein was found hiding in ad-Dawr, Iraq. He was arrested. The Ace of Spades was no longer a threat. Operation Red Dawn was a success, thanks in great part to Delta Force.

Hussein was found hiding in a hole near a farmhouse where he had been staying.

# CHAPTER 2

# BEFORE
## DELTA FORCE

**U**S Army Colonel Charles Beckwith was a Green Beret and a military advisor. In the early 1960s, he was an exchange officer with the British Special Air Service (SAS). Beckwith was impressed with the SAS's training, skills, and capabilities.

At the time, US Army Special Forces were trained for **unconventional warfare**. They were not trained for direct action

Colonel Charles Beckwith

or **counterterrorism**. Beckwith realized that the US military needed a unit like the SAS. His vision was to create a small group of highly trained men. It would be an **elite** force that could operate **undercover**. The men could work independently or as a team.

This was a completely new idea for the army. Men were typically trained to act as a team. They looked to their superiors for direction. Beckwith wanted men who liked working alone and could operate on their own. They had to be strong-minded and totally **dedicated** to success.

When Beckwith first proposed his ideas, his superiors were not convinced. After all, the army already had the Green Berets and the Army Rangers. They didn't believe it was necessary to create another special operations force. Then things changed.

The British SAS was created in 1941 to fight in World War II.

# CHAPTER 3

# A NEW
# THREAT

**B**efore the 1970s, **terrorism** was not a word that came up very often in the United States. The nation was well defended and its citizens felt safe. They never expected international acts of violence to affect them.

During the 1970s, things changed. Acts of terror became a serious problem in Europe and the Middle East. The US military realized it would not be long before terrorism hit home.

A key terrorist **strategy** is to attack **civilians** by surprise.

Kidnapping, **hostage** taking, and airplane **hijacking** were methods **terrorists** used.

In 1972, Palestinian **militants** attacked Israeli athletes and coaches at the Summer Olympic Games in Munich, West Germany. The events were seen on international television. People were shocked and changed forever. They could no longer feel as safe as they once did. This was a new threat and it wasn't going to go away soon.

It was time for the US military to learn how to fight terrorism. The US needed specially trained people who could fight and stop terrorists. It was time for Delta Force.

**One of eight terrorists who kidnapped and killed 11 Israelis during the games**

# CHAPTER 4

# DELTA
# FORCE
## IS BORN

In 1974, Beckwith was given the task of creating a special unit to respond to **terrorism**. He based his concept on his experience with the British SAS. He called the new unit Delta Force.

In his **memoir**, *Delta Force*, Beckwith wrote about his vision for the unit. He thought it should have small teams. Team members should be mature, professionally trained men. This was not

**General Edward Meyer**

a unit for a person who had just joined the army. The men needed to be mentally prepared to make quick, smart decisions.

Delta Force would include two groups. The first group was the operators. They were the men who performed the dangerous missions. The second group was the **administrators**. They supported the operators. Medical **personnel**, intelligence experts, and communications **specialists** were part of the administrative group.

General
Robert Kingston

Beckwith developed the plan with General Robert Kingston and General Edward Meyer. In the summer of 1977, they presented a formal proposal. It was approved and recommended for immediate action. On November 21, 1977, US Army First Special Forces Operational Detachment–Delta was officially created. Beckwith was chosen to be the commander.

# CHAPTER 5

# WHAT IS
## DELTA FORCE?

**D**elta Force was created to fight **terrorism**. To do this, operatives **disrupt** terrorist activities and capture or kill terrorists. One of their most important functions is to gather information about terrorist plots. With the right information, they can stop terrorists from carrying out their deadly plans.

The men of Delta Force are an **elite** group. They have the best training, weapons, and **technology** of any unit in the US military. They are the best of the best. They have to be. The job **guarantees** that they will be in close contact with the enemy.

Delta Force operators perform other roles besides **counterterrorism**. They also rescue **hostages**, protect government leaders, and perform dangerous **raids** and secret missions. The operators work alone or in small teams. They often need to make decisions on the spot.

Delta Force is a secret organization. Details about missions and operations are not shared with the public. Delta Force reports only to the highest military and intelligence officials, including the president. For Delta Force to be effective, its operatives have to stay hidden.

Delta Force operatives rely on their training and each other to accomplish their missions.

# CHAPTER 6

# JOINING
## DELTA FORCE

**Y**ou can't sign up or apply for Delta Force. You have to be **recruited**. Recruits must be male, already in the army, and at least 21 years old. No one with a rank lower than staff sergeant is recruited. Then there is a selection process. More than 90 percent of the recruits will drop out during selection.

The selection process is extremely physically and mentally challenging. No one is informed of the schedule or activities ahead of time.

The Modular Lightweight Load-carrying Equipment (MOLLE) rucksack can be adjusted for different loads.

Trainers make sure the recruits do pull-ups correctly.
They also count how many pull-ups the recruits complete.

For some men in the military, this is very upsetting. They are used to having a plan and a set schedule to follow.

Physical fitness is tested with timed running, push-ups, pull-ups, sit-ups, and swimming. But the most difficult tests are the rucks. A ruck is a long, fast walk while carrying a heavy rucksack. If **recruits** can't complete the ruck within the time limit, they won't move on. But they aren't told what the time limit is! They have to do their best and hope they make it.

There are two main rucks. The first is an 18-mile (29 km) ruck at night carrying 35 pounds (16 kg). The second is a 40-mile (64 km) ruck over rough, steep **terrain** carrying 45 pounds (20 kg).

Finally, the candidates undergo **psychological** testing and a thorough interview. And then, for just a handful of men, it's time to begin the real training.

# CHAPTER 7

OPERATOR

# TRAINING
## COURSE

The Operator Training Course (OTC) teaches skills operators need to perform their missions. The teachers include **snipers**, weapons **specialists**, and **demolitions** experts. Some instructors consult convicted burglars and

Snipers use special tools to check the wind speed and other conditions that can affect a shot.

escape artists and include their knowledge in the course. If Delta Force operators are going to catch criminals, they need the criminals' skills.

The men become expert **marksmen** with both handguns and **sniper** rifles. They use a special shooting house to practice rescuing **hostages**. The men take turns being hostages and rescuers. They use live **ammunition**, and the risk of being injured or killed is real.

Sometimes hostages are kept on upper floors of buildings. Delta Force operators are trained to climb with ropes to reach them.

Delta Force operators learn to use explosives to blow up buildings and bridges. They learn how to open any kind of lock without a key. These include doors, windows, cars, padlocks, and handcuffs.

The **tradecraft** portion of the training covers spy skills. The men learn how to observe people and situations, and how to gather information. They are taught how to pass secret information to other operators. They learn about secret signals and how to move without being seen. For the final test, they adapt and apply all the skills they have learned.

# READING A MAP

Orienteering is an important part of training. It **involves** finding your way somewhere using a compass and a map. Orienteering exercises usually take place in the wilderness. The candidates are given a topographic map. It shows the features of the land, such as mountains, valleys, lakes, rivers, and swamps.

A topographic map also shows elevation. Contour lines indicate the elevation. Each contour line equals a certain height. The closer the contour lines are to each other, the steeper the slope.

## LOOK FOR THE FOLLOWING FEATURES ON THE MAP

- A river
- A lake
- A building

- A road
- A trail
- The highest point

- The steepest slope
- Where a road crosses a river

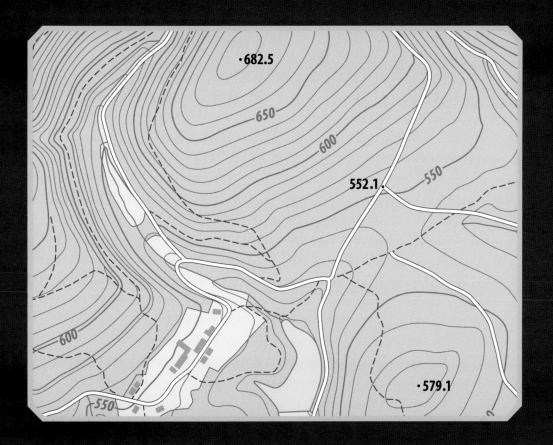

LEGEND

Building    Lake    Road

River    Trail    Elevation in feet

# CHAPTER 8

# SHADOW
## WARRIORS

**I**nformation about Delta Force is highly **classified**. Delta Force operators cannot tell anyone that they are in Delta Force. They sign a contract promising not to ever talk about what they do. They can't even tell their families.

Delta Force operators are anonymous and are trained to blend in with their surroundings. Because they work quietly and are seldom seen, they are sometimes called Shadow Warriors.

Delta Force is unusually informal compared to the rest of the army. The operators can dress casually in **civilian** clothing. They can grow beards and have long hair. The rule in the army is to address another person using their rank. For example, "Good afternoon, Sergeant Major." Delta Force operators often use nicknames for each other instead. This helps protect their anonymity.

A Delta Force operator isn't interested in recognition or fame. The army doesn't provide any information about their missions, locations, or identities. Once a man is accepted, he is considered **undercover**.

If he is killed in action, a cover story is invented to explain his death. The cover story makes sure that no details about any mission are made public. Officially, the government claims that Delta Force doesn't exist.

Delta Force operators are often required to blend in with the crowd.

# DELTA FORCE MISSIONS

Some Delta Force missions have been declassified. This means that they are officially no longer secret.

### Operation Urgent Fury, 1983 (Grenada)

The United States invaded the island of Grenada and overthrew the Communist government.

### Operation Just Cause, 1989 (Panama)

The United States invaded Panama to capture President Manuel Noriega. He was accused of helping Columbian drug traffickers. Noriega is now in prison.

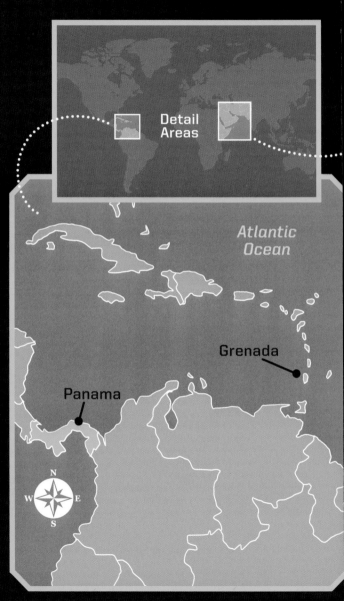

Detail Areas

Atlantic Ocean

Grenada

Panama

N W E S

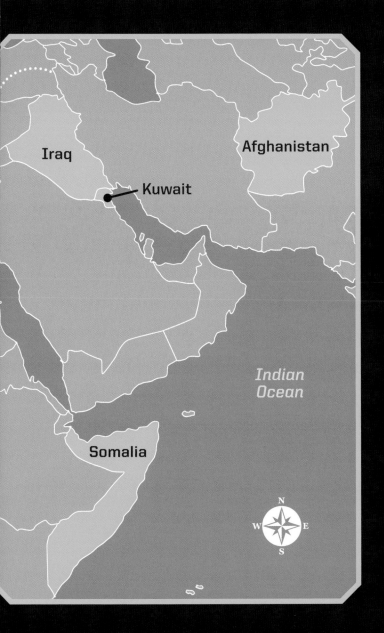

Iraq

Afghanistan

Kuwait

Indian
Ocean

Somalia

N
W · · E
S

## Gulf War, 1990-1991 (Kuwait)

Saddam Hussein's forces invaded and occupied Kuwait. Kuwait asked the United States and its **allies** to help free the nation from the Iraqi occupation.

## Operation Gothic Serpent, 1993 (Mogadishu, Somalia)

Delta Force operators and Army Rangers were sent to capture the Somali warlord Mohamed Farrah Aidid. Unfortunately, he escaped.

## Battle of Tora Bora, 2001 (Afghanistan)

The mission was to capture or kill Osama bin Laden. He was the leader of a group called al-Qaeda and mastermind of the 9/11 attacks. The al-Qaeda fighters were defeated, but it turned out that bin Laden was not there.

## Operation Red Dawn, 2003 (Iraq)

The hunt for Saddam Hussein.

# CHAPTER 9

# HEROES

It is rare for a Delta Force operator to be singled out for recognition. But two operators were given the Medal of Honor. It is the military's highest award. The US Congress votes to determine if someone should receive the Medal of Honor. Then the president presents it to the **recipient**.

Army Master Sergeant Gary Gordon

Army Sergeant First Class Randall Shughart

Delta Force operators Gary Gordon and Randall Shughart were **involved** in the Battle of Mogadishu in October of 1993. It happened at the end of Operation Gothic Serpent. Two Black Hawk **helicopters** had been shot down in Somalia. The Army Rangers were defending the site of the first crash. Hundreds of Somali fighters were rushing the second crash site. Gordon and Shughart knew the wounded crew could not survive on their own.

Using only their **sniper** rifles and pistols, they fought their way to the second downed helicopter. For a while, they were able to defend the helicopter and its crew. They fought bravely, but soon they were outnumbered and out of **ammunition**. Both men died that day. Their families received their Medals of Honor.

The US Army
Medal of Honor

# CHAPTER 10

# THE FUTURE OF DELTA FORCE

**D**elta Force is constantly adapting their tools and methods to work against new **terrorist** threats. Its operatives study and use the newest weapons, **technology**, and intelligence-gathering methods. Some of the technology and weapons they use are developed especially for their missions. They are already using the technology of the future. Some of it might never be known about or used outside of the military.

Most likely, there will be more focus on language and **cultural** skills. To operate successfully in a foreign country, operators need to speak the language. They often need to get cooperation from people in the countries where they serve. An understanding of the foreign culture is very important.

Soldiers use a language lab to practice Arabic. Today, it is the most common language taught to US soldiers.

Fighting terrorism is a full-time job, and Delta Force operators are dedicated to their work.

No one can say what the future will bring. For Delta Force operators, that's not a problem, it's an opportunity. From their first day of training they have learned to expect the unexpected. They keep their minds and bodies strong and their skills sharp. They keep their eyes wide open and all senses on alert. Whatever the future brings, these quiet heroes stand ready to protect and serve.

# TIMELINE

**1974**
US Army Colonel Charles Beckwith is given the task of creating a unit to respond to terrorism.

**1989**
Delta Force operators assist in the capture of Manuel Noriega in Panama.

**1990-1991**
Delta Force operators help free Kuwait from Iraqi occupation.

**1977**
US Army First Special Forces Operational Detachment-Delta is officially created.

**1983**
Delta Force operators participate in overthrowing the Communist government in Grenada.

**1993**
Gary Gordon and Randall Shughart die protecting a downed helicopter during the Battle of Mogadishu.

## 2001

Delta Force operators help defeat al-Qaeda forces in the Battle of Tora Bora.

## 2003

Delta Force operators are involved in the capture of Saddam Hussein.

# EXTREME FACTS

- Delta Force often allows foreign forces to take credit for its successful missions.

- The movie *Black Hawk Down* is based on a true story of a failed Delta Force mission.

- The television show *The Unit* was inspired by Delta Force.

- Delta Force operators are trained to shoot between heartbeats.

- A Delta Force operator can break into a car as fast as it can be opened with a key.

# GLOSSARY

**administrative** - related to managing a business, a school, or a government. A person who does this is an administrator.

**allies** - people, groups, or nations united for some special purpose.

**ammunition** - bullets, shells, cartridges, or other items used in firearms.

**civilian** - 1. a person who is not an active member of the military. 2. of or relating to something nonmilitary.

**classified** - kept from the public in order to protect national security.

**counterterrorism** - efforts and strategies to fight or prevent terrorism.

**culture** - the customs, arts, and tools of a nation or a people at a certain time. Something related to culture is cultural.

**dedicated** - committed to a goal or a way of life.

**demolition** - the act of destroying something, especially by using explosives.

**disrupt** - to throw into disorder.

**elite** - of or relating to the best of a class.

**guarantee** - to make sure or certain.

**helicopter** - an aircraft without wings. Instead, it has blades that rotate parallel to the ground.

**hijack** - to take over an airplane by threatening violence.

**hostage** - a person captured by another person or group in order to make a deal with authorities.

**imprison** - to put someone or something in prison.

**involve** - 1. to require certain parts or actions. 2. to take part in something.

# WEBSITES

To learn more about Special Ops, visit **booklinks.abdopublishing.com**. These links are routinely monitored and updated to provide the most current information available.

**marksman –** someone who is skilled at shooting a target.

**memoir** (MEHM-wahr) – a written account of a person's experiences.

**militant –** a person who is warlike or aggressively active in serving a cause.

**personnel –** a group of persons employed by a certain office or company.

**psychological –** related to someone's mind and behavior.

**raid –** a surprise attack.

**recipient –** someone who received something.

**recruit –** to get someone to join a group. A person who is recruited is called a recruit.

**sniper –** someone who shoots at an enemy from a hidden place far away.

**specialist –** someone who pursues one branch of study, called a specialty.

**strategy –** a careful plan or method.

**technology –** scientific tools or methods for doing tasks or solving problems.

**terrain –** the natural features of an area of land, such as mountains and rivers.

**terrorism –** the use of violence to threaten people or governments. A person who does this is a terrorist.

**tradecraft –** the techniques and procedures of espionage.

**unconventional warfare –** an attempt to achieve military victory through agreement, surrender, or spying.

**undercover –** acting in secret, such as spying.

# INDEX